the immediate excess poems

a. walther

Printed by CreateSpace, an amazon.com company

ISBN:0-9831776-1-9
ISBN-13:978-0-9831776-1-6

CONTENTS

alpha spark 1

this(?) is a poem? 3

the clockmaker...7

excerpt filling introjection..9

a clearing in the forest.. 11

a dream life 13

winter seams 15

scarlet ohio 17

a polynesian mirror.. 19

a blue perception 21

a sobering ego trip 23

saints like lennon.. 25

coloring outside the lines.. 27

bethlehem, 21st street 29

his reclining nude... 31

destiny doesn't need children 33

the blue grassroots.. 35

sketching miles via spain.. 37

craving ophelia... 41

a short tale from a midwestern womb 43

the good doctors were in.. 45

a limn rich in soda 47

a practical birth and those reborn 49

drawn from a dark room.. 55

the embodiment of 57

a slice of the universe.. 59

maker of rain/curator of light... 61

an avenue on harms way..63

the scythe swinging sermon...65

swimming upstream..67

same old sometimes or: life 101 69

legendarily perverse 71

a writer's blog 75

the proverbial paradise..77

the curse..79

opa..81

owning up...85

a collage and an 8-track...87

alternate ego eccentrics..91

van gogh deserving 93

television paint..95

native land/native trust..97

a speakeasy..99

the recurring theme of drink...103

sleep space 105

the cleanliness of film...107

proper channels..109

the three graces 111

omega moonlight 113

cid in america..115

burning bridges 119

eternal witness/constant observer 123

against the all-mighty...127

inside the box/balancing the scales..129

when in need 131

alpha spark

the night engulfs again

in all its metaphor

a shadow turning a silhouette

into the face of a poem

lost and then found

in the consuming twisted love of art.

this(?) is a poem?

a person who generally thinks about writing writes as a 'way of life'
or a way to 'pass the time'.
and although writing (like this) may be slightly more involved than
doodling, someone who likes to pass their time drawing cartoons or
comics – or doodling – can't help but wonder if they could somehow
achieve some significant financial gain if what they are doodling may
actually be humorous or inventive or thought provoking.
it's certainly part of our, present day, human nature to think financial gain.

thinking about art or doing art or contemplating art can drive people crazy –
in case you hadn't noticed.
it's kind of like trying to figure out the meaning of life; more
an explanation of itself, the writer and an example of art while trying
not to imitate, plagiarize or dwell on the meaning of
you know what.

a book need not be made-up of long, fancy poems.
it need not be fact or fiction.
it can be both; made-up of facts and ideas that we know can be true
or to be inevitably true (a form of life creating art and imitating life, in turn).

some, apparently, have learned the good to be found in 'poetic license'
deserving of a few liberties, minor alterations and embellishments
(see oliver stone, like him or not).

and if someone like james frey had just said his book was 'fiction'
he would never have 'hoodwinked' oprah, and his 'half-truths' about bits
and pieces of shit and fucked-up lives, everywhere, would have all
co-existed in scope and detailed perspective.
the people in frey's book knew who they were and what they represented,
at least the ones that survived the story.
after all – in a sense – isn't this what the majority of people do in their spare
personal time, anyways, to prove a point; to try and make themselves 'look'
better in the eyes of others?
whether it's a slight makeover, change in wardrobe, or a new job,
it's always something in the attempt to explain the kind of people
we all are; mostly fact; better fiction; for better or worse.

and boredom can become a necessary alternative to that vanity.
there is simplicity and safety in being good and bored; aka: bored
(practically) senseless; or 'bored to tears'.
there is little harm or damage being done (to others), only within;
and within is where good art is found and eventually visualized.
after all, art is life and life is art.
and life imitating art (in these eyes) is more stimulating
(yes, more self-gratifying) and more original – maybe even more creative –
than art imitating life.
art imitating life is a carbon copy of something like a picture
that has already been taken and then repainted.
it may look good, again, but that's all it is: a replica.
it has nothing to do with how the painter may see himself or other people;
or how he or she may be able to see clearly beyond the colors of a landscape
or some inanimate objects where the colors don't have to be 'right'.
it's a deception in perception that allows some artists the right and the
ability to see things differently in themselves –
and other possible artists –

that makes the picture or the painting or the sentence art;
that creates itself, art; or life imitating art.

ah,
the simple boring day
all by itself;
each breath valued
yet barely noticeable;
of once living the good life
while 'using the net';
of occasionally 'living large' even when this no longer means
or feels like forever.
sometimes, slow misery will slowly love you to acceptance
because it's no longer just your bored soul
allowing the perfect line in the perfect poem
to be thought of in a fantasy of fiction
so that no more books, songs or poems need to be written.
but, of course, that's ridiculous because everyone
who writes/writes for him or herself – good or not –
since perfection is out of the ordinary; out of the question.

artists just need to be understood,
a little bit, to fill that void
and fill that vein
with some sort of herb drink flower
or poetic drug
to consume the days
like visual stimulation needs to be seen
under somebody's egotistical terms
pleasuring, often, internally and efficiently
the perfect passive-aggressive wonderment.

the clockmaker

the clockmaker smiles when she needs;
feels her pain like his own;
holds her face in time and hand;

she is his spirit; he,
her carpenter building a home;
bound by the foundation
of their love;

and a baker of bread for the soul purpose
and the knowledge
of their growth and togetherness;

the hands of the clockmaker never slow,
yet grow stronger
with each motion;

revolving around her
with perfect timing
and the pride
he will continue to build for them
with a good carpenter's wood
something resembling a cross;

and

with their own flesh and blood

connecting to their souls

the absolution of a truth:

the self-taught man

is her practicing necessity.

excerpt filling introjection

i saw in some book or a movie or somewhere that t.s.eliot

wrote poetry to escape from emotion; and, that a down-on-his-luck writer –

often referred to, simply, as buk – writing in his crude,

yet modern poems and journals, said,

through the common sense of a woman,

that his 'greatest strength was his fear of everything'

and also (to buk's credit)

that a good poem says as much as possible in as short a period of time

as possible.

just about anybody could have said 'poetry *is* about emotion.'

mark twain supposedly said he could never 'write how he felt'

(very modest of samuel).

henry david thoreau observed man lives in 'quiet desperation'

(fair enough)

and even socrates knew 'i know that i know nothing'

(ingenious of him, i think).

many have said little

and even more too much.

that which is done out of love takes place beyond (nietzche's)

good and evil

(and it drove one of the greatest thinkers of any century

straight into a state of *catatonia*, wherever that hell(?) may be).

collectively, in art, the senses can be considered a singular entity

not plural.

the senses must be seduced before they can be taught the abstract.
and abstraction not confined
will always find a muse
defined to create an original forum
and discover a new temptation
(originality, new temptations, the senses and the artful pattern
 of abstract interests *are* sometimes difficult to describe and just as
 difficult to erase from any artist philanthropist philosopher).

a clearing in the forest

autumn approaches
teetering on the brink
of its own scheme
because even the seasons
question
in a period
why they have succumbed
to a black & white
theme

where a leaf separate from a branch
in a wilderness of static
shows a sign of aging
rings circling the core

yet very still
this pathos
and the path
well-traveled
down

leads to a brush of trees
in a paper wind
awakening
a color at the surface

with barely a wrinkle
of a sound in that breeze
succumbing to a time and a season:
in a blank revolution
trees still
do fall.

a dream life

a young man wanders
growing introspective
in a cartoon type world

listening to others expound
about their animated existential existence
in the most stimulating conversations
of their waking
dream state minds

each room
each face
a composite
of a moving
altered state
and constant motion

an active still life
the continuum of a portrait
explaining to a degree
the everlasting undying theme...

winter seams

the scene sets
on the center of town
in the middle of a midwestern snow
on the local blvd.;
a movie cinema closed for the night,
vacant;
a blue wind whipping through an alley in a swirl of snow dust;
the last cold breath taken by what remains of some green grass
barren as the peppered birch in the triangle by the gazebo;
and its approving natural struggle;

a neon bar across the street signs its tinted window,
advertising,
and the 'breakfast shoppe' next door opening at five;
the plaza parking lot covered in a thin white blanket alive
in the movement of light snow swirling like a helpless,
soulless ghost spinning in its transparent funnel
hovering, atop, the frozen surface
and disintegrating as it tries to elevate

as the first mechanical sound of the morning echoes in
mankind, approaching,
rumbling from down the street
and spraying a thin wave of dark snow over the curb
(in passing);

winter seams
in the early morning night
connecting
the fall from the black sky whitening grey
as a nova-cluster warm themselves in their untouchable distance
reveling in their own minor tempest
a faceless timeless hint of possibilities.

scarlet ohio

a late november sky
cast in clay
does not seem
finished.
it has dampened
the color spectrum
(that we tend to look for)
of another day
with another grey dawn;
a perfect match
to the cement earth.

rarely dry, on these days,
the midwesterner tends to appear
on land in dress
wearing turtlenecks
and weathered boots,
just a december step aside
from a near frozen black creek

where the midwest image of winter
is picture-postcard sleigh driven;
in worship of evergreens; and
a soft snow falling in the yard

of a covered hillside;
a vision of buckeyes at play in the field;

and a well-lit rural home
in a scene from the dawn of the century
dusting the holiday season
with the feel good remnants of a new year.

a polynesian mirror

the loss of creation is felt

in the comfort zone of the tv and a biography special

watching the artist

to be

'run away from it all':

the wife the kids the job

and the stilted waste of convention

no longer restricting in a place like tahiti and its

canvas landscapes;

reborn on an island and its water colors and paint

all the while

reminiscing in a tropical polynesia

of a breton homeland

where the simplest pleasures mattered

in the end

to gauguin

in wake of a classic promiscuous death

on one island universe

of self-portraits and native lands

wading into personal reflections

pacific and blue.

a blue perception

the ocean lies quiet at dawn

as a two thousand year-old wave

rolls to the shore and breaks in a rippled pitch

with another   and another

and the open air surrounding the ancient sea

supplies its own vast restriction

upon movement

as the tide straightens the silence

within the semblance of a day

and sunlight bathing on the surface

of familiar sound

ranging farther

from the singular fathom of a lake depth,

percepted.

a sobering ego trip

a light slips through a window
blind,
in its way,
in standard delay of night.

any man has the vision to see
what is bred
or born to be
from a puritan upbringing
christian
to the godless peaceful soul
nowhere near
the complex
jesus.

people are born the same
and of the same insight:
the belief that man lives
for one another

and not sin

resurrecting

for love of man;

and *his* fear of living

becoming (as it is) temptation

and eternal consciousness

forgiving only those

who belong to 'the club'

without question

of right or wrong.

saints like lennon

wouldn't the greatest artist be the person
who doesn't need to paint or sculpt
or write or direct
anything resembling an act?

the greatest artist would
in affect
create nothing outside of a selfless
quiet song that all could recognize
while indulging in nothing
but life
without hesitation
regret or despair.

coloring outside the lines

is it a flaw to be an expert of nothing?

inside, is all the matter
of what it's all about;

the pauses from within
to ridicule and reason:
the senses should
soften with age
as simply

as the sight of her, one day;
clear as a summer sky, the next,
and the way she feels,
warm;
slightly more complicated
than a touch;

a preamble
echoing
the eternal guardians
of instinct
and the relativity
of a smile;

and kudos to
the victors over
the quiet battles won;
the basis of a few
respectful
child-like words
open for suggestion

and,
an after thought…

and love and sex
as stimulating
as consenting
hearts

can hope for;
asking fewer questions
and asking for far less,
in return

striving for no more necessities.

bethlehem, 21st street

it must have all imploded
on this day,
or so it may have seemed,
for those who live(d) there;

the guns spinning on their turrets
set on the tv news:
a simple image of men
expendable for attrition's sake

blasting kingdom come
towards another birth
and reign
of martyrdom.

was there ever a symbol
of peace

once upon a starry night...?

or was it always a fairy tale –
the christ drum beating itself
with the addition of a naive little boy –
in a god forsaken season of the desert.

is it too late to allow children
to play with a creation
they have not learned
to believe in?

his reclining nude

desire burns within the *dying animal*
yet somehow
in someway
it does not understand
exactly
why it is struck, endlessly,
by the lucent pose
of an amadeo spectra

as she extends in our privacy
the faintness of a smile,
in the length of her profile;
eyes closed
relying on the very color of our being

because even the aged animal
should realize,
if nothing else,
he is fooling
absolutely
nobody.

destiny doesn't need children

it's easy for artists to become too serious with themselves
while trying to discover their voice or their muse;
in the company of the familiar rhetoric of fancy words
muddled by length and abstraction,
like henry miller at his creative worst;
or a near sighted van gogh attempting to love
beyond his paint and his canvas creation;
not in disgust – like a pissing disorienting picasso –
at the sight of heterosexual women;

unable to avoid the obvious preconceptions;
or the truest sense of realities futility
forcing indifference upon emotion
and attempting the execution of conformity;

a painter's attempt to preview and analyze
an everyday of orgy;
or not warning or praising what time can do
like a – vonnegut (and so on) – novelty
with the cheeky-ass humor;

as, eventually, off comes an ear
or a prick or a writer's tit
all for one poverty enriched, conceited original vision
or voice;
the flaw of sanity sterilizing,
but not cleansing,
for the artist who seems to be working hard
at nothing;
weak yet stronger creatively than ever
in a sudden temporal brush with madness
and a temporary
transitory stroke of ego and immoral genius.

not everybody wants kids
yet most want to fuck.

all and all,
visceral golden virtues and
silvered tendencies at best
weigh in as potency
in wonderment:

is this the way the painting should be
or just a sign of things to come?

the blue grassroots

to know a bad poem when (you) see it
(or write it) is to get the joke, for starters.

understanding is the child who knows
behavior is to be friendly; that it is not
an offering to be polite and forgiving to those
who are participating in our brand new lives.
it's natural and fair to give anyone a chance.
this may explain why a child can become stricken
with the fear of being left alone:
where is everyone you know? even a stranger
doesn't look bad as long as it is a familiar,
friendly face with a nose, eyes and a smile.

it is an 'event' and the inevitable chronology
that challenges youthful exuberance.

it turns out the grass is not always green
the sky is not always blue
and the landscape seems to survive with the, somehow,
fruitful combination of a few grainy notes;
a precursor of 'the blues'
that flows from a knowing gospel
with or without a church

with lyric like molasses
dripping forward, with a taste,
of the whiskey river's
valuable ruin;
and the bed beneath the beating heart
of the child within.

sketching miles via spain

picasso should have liked
this style of music, if he didn't.
these, earlier, turn of the century composers
were loyal
to the heart of
their land;

a spaniard's french horn
and a flute, mourning,
a sad yet, somehow,
hopeful note;
an odd combination
indeed
improvising these styles
with the accompaniment
that registers
on the penny whistle
his trumpet speak

and the strings, imagined;
in the orange and red spain
of a woodwind orchestra
warming to the calibrating
sun;

of a procession, highlighting,
the rising crescendo
for a
stain pewter crucifix
on display for the crowd
on a village road
building a place

alongside the
redemption peace.

    part 2 live: berlin

ice softens in a golden tumbler
marked by humid condensation
sliding slowly –
one, two seconds apart –
two droplets clear and content;

silence segues
before the next bronze close-up
sends miles through his looking-glass
warming to the 'visionaries'
listening
by the temperate feel
of the attitude
of a 'cool' setting;
the version continuing
on a stage lit
on cue
smooth

as 'a stick' of atmosphere's
placement
burns softly;

the circles viewing
in line
of the music's
mathematic
precision;

a piano key kisses
the applause;
the taste remnants

tapping, tapping into
the symbol in speed of
the beat;
miles in front
and ahead;

a picture
of the foreground
burning, just so lightly,
in the powdered ash

that rest
in the host
of these
small masses.

craving ophelia

all it takes is the sound
of an ophelia
and you're hooked.
but, as with most that seems good,
you should, always, pause
to stop
and relive any
false excess;

and re-examine
and vegetate yourself
and pay the cost
of the lowly downside
of any reckless
obsession;

observing
as the
ophelian onion unfolds
as sweet and grand
and tragic
as the mood of an out-dated, italian opera
or the memory of a shakespearean play –

and the relevance of romeo and juliette
in junior high school
while a car radio plays a tragic love song
from the too late 1970's.

hamlet would stab himself in the back
(albeit polonius)
because of
something to do with
far too many play thing
obsessions
and being a prince.

et tu claudius.

a short tale from a
midwestern womb

there seems to be some reason for

an apology

to all those struggling artists

who suffered, in their way:

pollock, pinero, basquiat,

these 'modern day' painters and poets

living, it would seem, in the truest sense

of the artist's process,

on their own and alone

on poverty streets strife

with their addictive ease;

whores all by themselves

and infidels to the idea

of being alive;

sparing very brief preservations

of compromise;

the score of the art, for sure,

company secured –

of miseries –

in the force and the rush, needed,

for success

and the impurity to escape

naïvete

as personally as possible
even if not ready or convenient.
it seems even william blake knew of this
before aldoux huxley and the whole
'doors of perception' conception.
so,
there's an apology for little travel
and not so much filthy experience
living in a suburb in the midwest
where there are bare tree necessities
on a street littered in a familiar state
of mind; nothing fancy, for sure,
or drastic;
just another march in ohio
and a grey horizon setting
easily watching that yellow sun
go down as usual –
sometimes orange
sometimes in red.

the good doctors were in

it's not surprising fundamentalists hated him
and the religious zealots too; with his drink
in one hand and a blue micro dot in the other
it was quite apparent he could care less
what most people thought about him
as long as he was able to write and be heard.

more than once i could not help but wonder
how much of my own admiration for his style
and success was actually envy.
but, it was difficult not to appreciate the humor and
disgust that tore at the man right down to his
bowels; the madmen politicians coupled with the
booze and the gambling, and the other extremes
and excesses right down to the savage drug intake;
and enjoying the hunt; and, somehow, managing
to remain the sanest of the lot while hallucinating
and melding within the insanity surrounding him
(at least it seemed to work for the 'good doctor').

i did not know the man, personally, but he certainly
left an indelible impression right down to the wardrobe:
the safari hat and large sunglasses; the long
cigarette-filter; the slacks and the sneakers.

but, even he could not just fade-out...
he pulled-out his hemingway
and went out the hard way.
or was it the easy way?
it's another question razed by a man who brought us a
helluva' mind and the controversy that went with it.

* * *

a philosopher named epicurus – who lived before christ
was born – believed we should live unseen and unheard,
and that we had two basic fears: fear of gods and fear of
death; and epicurus kind of made it his job to convince
people there was no need to fear anything…just be happy!
imagine this, and before christianity too
(maybe not much of a revelation but what the hell).
the people back then, who didn't think epicurus was crazy,
probably thought he was a good mind doctor.
he probably had a following (sounds kind of familiar) and,
as far as i know, he was never strung-up somewhere and
left to die as a heretic and did not do himself-in in any way,
shape or self-mutilation.
they probably smoked some good herb or clove back in those
days and i'm guessing they had some form of fermented drink
to sip and vice on; in the hope and the hype that some good,
mellow smoke and mild drink would help in a simpler time;
that a land devoid of political deceptions, deceitful evangelists,
and the general craziness and mayhem that appears to run
rampant across this beloved globe of ours might not seem an
impossibility or a revelation.
anyways, just a thought.

a limn rich in soda

from every soft, sweet taste is
revealed a natural pre-conception...

innocence revealed
on the face of a summer weekend;
rainbow sherbet scooped from the bin
from behind the sliding glass;
teenagers sipping on their first
wine cooler during summer break.
my we grow-up fast.

there should be a boycott of boycotts,
starting with the olympics;
an appreciation for the old-fashioned
and the standards;
international futbol;
the world series;
german, czech, and belgian ales, bottled;
actual peace on a national holiday;
international holidays;
never a stereotype of the open-minded;
lesbian love, naturally;
heterosexual fantasies, in general.

in a not too controlled, trouble-free environment
miscegenation is a libertine movement;
purely exotica...

so the remnant nature of a melting-pot
may feel and taste sweet for whoever
may indulge in acquiring the need
for something
different from the usual.

a practical birth and those reborn

i'd spent the night at a recently acquainted friend's house
talking about working together; and watching tv
with her husband.
in the morning we went to their daughter's youth soccer game
on a colder than cool day in april.
the kids wandered around the field in tight little packs
some faster and some kicking the ball harder than others.
fewer, still, wandered a little less decisive and, certainly,
less restless in their own little world.

after the game ended it was their son's turn.
two years older than his sister i would've liked to see the
baseball game but it was 'clear on the other side of town.'
i had a few hours to spare before i was, basically,
forced to go to work – which was nearby – and since
the parents had some time between games, also,
i suggested buying breakfast at a local
denny's restaurant for them
and maybe their third child, a two-year-old daughter.
a minor mistake in a bachelor's world.
we soon joked how fortunate and wise i'd been never to have
children – 'that i knew of, ha ha' – as she crawled under the table and
cried her pancakes had been cut wrong and, eventually, bounced

around the line at the cashier's counter like a little pinball with hands
trying to grab hold of any and everything at her eye level.

being proud, responsible parents they, of course, refused my offer to pay
for their breakfast, so i paid for my own and insisted on leaving the 15%
tip, and they agreed.
i wished them 'good luck' as they tried to strap the two year-old in her car
seat – squirming and wining – and they reminded me 'we warned you,'
which they had and i was surprised they smiled and reasoned
they were used to her outbursts and displays of public attention.
i stepped back and watched what was the end of our day together.
'oh, quiet down,' her daddy said, 'it's not that bad.'
the older brother sat – arms folded, waiting – in their suburban caravan.
the middle child laughed, next to her brother; her game was over.

and we went our separate ways.
i stayed close to work, driving to a cvs store to buy a toothbrush and
toothpaste, a bottle of mineral water and a small bottle of listerine.
i was on somewhat of a mission to repel the lingering taste of stale
beer from the night before coupled with the immediate dry manifestations
of morning breath and the greasy current of bacon, eggs, and hash browns
with coffee and juice;
the cranberry juice the only deterrent resembling a wash.

i parked the car in a mostly empty parking lot and went to work
disinfecting my mouth.
i gargled, copiously, with the listerine until it burned my cheek gums raw,
and spit the remaining lukewarm liquid judiciously out the window.
i had bought the old-fashioned bottle of listerine out of reputation because

i was not concerned about a 'minty' taste, but a freshness; an undeniably
clean and 'mediciney' finish.
i liked the old-fashioned commercial, no-nonsense, cardboard-paper layered
and wrapped around the short, pudgy bottle
with the small black cap.
the yellow and the ugly mustard brown of the listerine packaging, somehow,
looked good together, and the piss-colored liquid seemed to speak for itself.
i gave a nod to andy warhol for saying the campell's soup can was art.
i was a.walther agreeing the packaging could be art;
the camel red cigarette box, also, was art.
but, i refused to light one.
the pudgy listerine bottle – and that yellow antiseptic – was a phallic
reminder that fit perfectly in the palm of my hand, and i laughed at myself
for dribbling the liquid down my chin,
absorbing in the shadow of what remained
in the stubble of my goat tee.
i wiped the wet-itch from my chin and then proceeded to brush the remains
of my cruddy and neglected, day-old-teeth with doctor sheffield's
baking soda toothpaste.
i used the bottled spring water to moisten the chalky paste on the
toothbrush; swigged water; and a swish of listerine
from the black cap
(a tough poor i, probably, shouldn't have wasted the time to do since
 since some spillage was, practically, unavoidable and wasteful).
i spit again, refreshed, and glanced at dr. sheffield's baking soda toothpaste
realizing they had been the original toothpaste producers.
it said so on their simple white box.
i had not known that.

and then, sometimes, you realize you have nothing to do but something
to prove besides attending the workplace, although you pretty much have no
choice.
somewhat luckily, earlier in the week, i had checked-out a book from the
library and had left it in the car on the passenger's seat because, sometimes,
'you never know'.
it was a memoir titled *7 tattoos* about a man raised in the jewish faith
who began to question his born religion – gasp! especially from a
man who was taught that self-mutilation involves tattoos
(jesus never had a tattoo) and found answers to his questions
and beliefs through
the demonstration of body art; and for each tattoo there was a story
explaining why it existed on his body and the faith it helped restore in
himself and his family.
i read for about half-an-hour, with the window down, the sun beating on the
windshield; slowly baking the interior despite the brisk, april air; the
right side of my body becoming warmer than the left, cooled by my arm –
like a conductor – my temperate elbow perched on the open,
driver's side window; my fingertips tapping the top of the doorframe.
i had to adjust in my seat, propping the book against the steering
wheel as i continued to read about a man's life that was, basically,
more interesting than mine; of his political suspicions and
inevitable distrust; personal misgivings and loves lost;
and the self-deprecating humor needed to keep yourself
honest.
and my ass began to get sweaty from the right-sided heat.
i'm sometimes easily distracted.
and i began to get anxious; beginning to wonder if six beers drunk
late at night – within a few hours – and then two cups of coffee with
a greasy breakfast the next morning might have an adverse effect
on themselves and, of course, me; convincing myself a heart attack

was not implausible; too many, daily, six-packs; not enough sleep

from too much coffee; not enough decaf; not enough writing;

and there was a good chance i should not be late for work

a third time in the same year.

and the sudden thought of never getting a book published

began to scare the shit out of me!

there would be absolutely nothing to remember me by

in any form of braggadocio or posterity sake!

it would be like i never existed; snipped, gone!

i took a deep breath and recovered quickly enough;

thought about

her naked body and her – embarrassing to her – stretch marks.

'they're not that bad,' i had told her – a mother of three.

she did not believe like some would insist we'd had an affair.

it was innocent enough, anxiety be told.

and i had to leave the parking lot

with nothing to do

but drive to work

and perform a customer service duty

and not be a minute too late.

drawn from a dark room

the blinds split but,
still, the opening
is lined in pitch;
of a natural science
awakening outside
to the shadows
thriving within;
fluttering walls,
blanketing movement –
outside the exhale
 of the wind
suggests a minutiae
 within the hints
of that whispering flow;

of a darkness
on the inside
blanketing peace;
a blanket of mind;

a preparation
itself
involving
a fashion;

the night
forgiving the day
of its seeds;
welcoming darkness

subdued and tame as the
rarely seen;
only remembered;

but felt in the adjustment
to such a cover
of darkness
over light.

the embodiment of

it can be difficult to write
when it's all in the head
and not on the paper,
yet (always yet);
when the references and personal
examinations come full-circle
and the writer's purpose and motive
become seriously questioned:
is he just becoming a 'shrink'
to his own psychoses?
well, yes.

only the mind can envision
or the eyes can touch
the embodiment of a poem
before it happens,
in proper;
(a pausing)
that the pure love of anything or anyone
is golden silence.
it may be the highest point of cessation
in any circle of temples and saints
who are just being 'of themselves'
in a group denomination;

avoiding strife and turmoil
while accepting 'others'
and the fault of the individual;

just to be a part of the natural,
living piece of life
and all that it embodies.

a slice of the universe

the editors have a habit of returning the book,
as requested.
poems don't bode well for an undergrad.

all the same, sometimes the mind has not matured
beyond science fiction and vampire fables.

and the underdog is alive and doing *too* well
in other stories of fiction.

'you sure do have a way with women,' she said.
it was a kiss of death; and nothing else was said.
and she wasn't even an editor; not accepting
poetry submittals, to say the least.

the slice started as a slit.

'what part didn't you like? the purple and red nebulae –
within the acknowledgment of life itself – pulsating in a
quiet tempest; stars warming in a current of light and a,
suddenly, penetrable conclusion to the mystery of
consciousness; forgiving the infinite before the acceptance
of extreme momentum slamming to a halt?'

she didn't – seem – to acknowledge; not even quizzically.
she calmly averted her eyes and waited.
he said nothing more.

'see you later?' she finally said, asking, out of the polite
necessity that still remained in her nature.
'probably,' he answered.

the universe continues to hesitate and grow.
it is space wide and open within all its astronomical
growth and wisdom and maturation.
it should be a place to rest under and sleep within,
free; freedom's choice of soul perfection
within a human universe, of course; a red star
red blooded extravaganza; a visceral enhancing
galaxy in flux of vision and understanding.

'i didn't appreciate the red and purple pulsating slit,'
she said. 'i know what you mean.'

'yeah, but, what about the rest of the universe...
 being...?' whatever.

maker of rain/curator of light

it is lightness and the like
falling at the rate of a,
slowly, spinning wheel
revolving in a mist and sun
and neon-violet rain

borrowing, heavily,
from a primitive chronology
before age and beauty
were lost;

in an arc of colors
reaching out
touching the likeness
and the light, seeking;
always seeking
to join in
on the instrument
of its own vitality;

no fear
of a vision,
thumping softly;
building to another crescendo

beating, settling soft and sound
like notes falling
in volume quicker,
a pace stronger
toward the contact;

the rhythm chiming-in;
the water – fall and fluid.

an avenue on harms way

we stand, together,
in the lap of, this,
suburban america
and a, rather, knowledgeable
expectation of each other.

we have the inordinate ability
not to harm, intentionally.
there is much less trauma,
all around,
directed at the one's we know, personally;
for the middle class in the midwest
are the 'unlucky' when accosted
by strangers – at the wrong place
at the wrong time; thankful
for the character of the people
we tend to know, see,
and relate to, somewhere,
on a daily basis.

the scythe swinging sermon

(one minute an observer and witness
 and the next
 the unmitigated victim
 of ridiculous circumstance –
 an undeniable addition, this is, to the 'unlucky')…

a scythian rebirth
regales aversions/envisioned in
such familiar flight;
a permanence in its power-hungered
flailing notions;
bending over the terrain like new;
pulsating in its
dominance and population;
living in the decadent glory
and name that reaps
its own tool and its own blade;

in accordance with
themselves in black,
the sea
and its regents.

swimming upstream

everyone has a dream,
or did;
a river of hope;
a stream of consciousness, even;
one of a thousand cliché's
pulled – not necessarily all that deep –
from the heart
or the soul;

an expression that inspires actors:
one-half artist one-half exhibitionist;
idea and thought born from a carnival
of personality traits and their
'character study' of mounting
complexities.

others learn at the cost
of unwritten letters or
never conceived poems
colored, immeasurably,
by age and the belated
wisdom of
living and learning.

dreams remain
in a veil of experience;
and luck follows:
born the same
but raised differently,
downstream;
rarely by choice;

and creativity discussed
like a mute topic;
a refusal of its own inspiration,
it seems,
in this day and age
of formal currency;
barely a mention
in terms of wealth;

an easy consolidation
of all that is good
and poor;

and the mind to surround itself
in its own daily streams.

same old sometimes or: life 101

sometimes, i gets in the way.
'same old bullshit, different day'
is selfish boredom, sometimes.
sometimes different from
person to person
not knowing what to like,
who to like, or when to like.
it's a slump of sorts
that should not last.
it may get worse when
drink and masturbation
go hand-in-hand
and, after a while,
are no longer fun,
together.
and, being told,
you can't catch-up on sleep.
depressing, disagreeing
a tired boredom lingers
heavily on a soul, weighed
and anchored, dropping low
on a heavy heart; more mental;
then physical, for the time
being; breathing, not so

becoming; a peek at an abyss
filled with self-loathing;
the crack in the demeanor explores
before, eventually, revealing a
crack in the smile for a show
of hands not caring – that much;
a change in the reminder of how
things used to be; the selfish 'i'
forgetting not to miss
the color in the day;
the blues and the greens and
the calm breeze and the warm sun;
understanding simplicity;
the appreciation for the understated
as control returns
taking the rat race for what it is:
a maze in a game to speed-up through
and get around.
it's just the temporary pace of the
population, in overdrive; a time for
integrating all with little or no exaggerated
hatred or fear.
and, sometimes, it can last
for more than a day.

legendarily perverse

it's been written that sweet little emily dickinson
lived – and may have loved – a perverse lifestyle.
doesn't seem possible, does it?
but, consider this: we are told she rarely strayed
from her home in amherst, massachusettes
which makes her sound like a recluse or a homebody;
eccentric, maybe; but perverse?
what was going on with her and the clergyman
the family was supposedly very close to in their day?
perverse eh?
makes one wonder if emily was harboring a dildo in 1854?

she, apparently, lived in a nice section of a well-to-do town.
the locals that had successful businesses knew her successful
father whose family was directly responsible for founding
their hometown of amherst.
it may have been an absolutely lovely arrangement
for the dickinson family.
her brother lived right next door with his wife but, apparently,
poor perverted emily didn't do much; she never traveled much;
just stayed at home like an 'old maid'; only becoming famous
after she died for writing some simple, mostly rhyming poetry.
she did have the privilege of seven published poems while
alive, so that may have been cause for fun and celebration.

she probably lived well within the family's wealth, with some
token misery; basically alone with the solitude – and the stepping
stone of ideas that balanced along with it;
of how to feel and become
comfortable writing within her own skin so that others – in their not so
perverse lifestyle – might want to read and relate.
emily had the occasional companion, male we assume;
good for the soul; knowing full well she was alive in a
dull time and place just trying to get by ignoring death
the best way she could.
emily was never part of some great revolution involving murders,
deceit, politics or religion.
she seemed to avoid the temptations of madness.
it was just a quiet revolution within herself, if you will.
she was, apparently, sociable when people were around.
sometimes, a safe haven and minimal involvement help
provide longevity with a roof and four walls.
what else is really necessary, could emily have figured?
she lived under god's creation in general
with access to a museum of books.
the dickinson family did what it wanted,
in the town of amherst.
they were its pioneers.
and emily was perverse, in her lifestyle, because of it.
did emily dickinson ever look-up the word 'perverse'
in her volumes?
wonder if she ever considered herself
in that manner; or an existentialist; or a
closet nihilist, if nothing else
other than perverse?

emily elizabeth dickinson lived to be 56.
not much of an old maid after all, although that probably
seemed older back in 1886.
still, so much for longevity for the quiet and subversive;
and for believing in the
apple pie of someone when words have more than one
meaning we innocently –say, maybe even perversely –
had become accustomed to.
golly, how perverse it all is.

a writer's blog

he hoped to write something concrete
in his novel books.
the thought of *writing from a hungover suburb*
seemed to garner some laughs while
the whipping circle fell by the darker wayside.
but, there was little beyond a starting point and a
good chapter here and there.
and he, soon, more than once, would tell himself:
you're not a writer at all; you can't make
the time and you don't have the patience.
where's the inspiration and the drive?
the voice that must be heard
if only by one or two or other writers?
why can't it be done, again, your way?

always, it seems, barely hanging-on
by tidbits of this and that;
knick-knacks to a slowly probing network
of brainwaves sliding sideways
with age; the ancient souls of so many
borrowing from antique religions
come and gone to the fore;
the big front;

common sense reincarnated
from centuries ago;
the spirit of the temples within;

god as law preserving morality;
simply a time
simply void
of most reason
like popular decadence as fashion
and currency becoming the only art
form;
the modernization of the forming
state;
and the future sanctioned
on the solipsist as he does
his best
to relieve himself of his emotion
and re-observe from the outside
in;
even if he is
just a 'has been' reborn,
agnostic and/or sexist.

the proverbial paradise

paradise is at the heart;
a space where fear does not exist;
pain and mortality more a rumor than a factor,
far, far away;
a place where the soul
sets on the nirvana
of a wine burgundy light;
and the moments of absolute clarity
undaunted, and seamless, and
free of limits,

it would seem.
until a fool emerges
in one form or another
not aware of the possibilities
or the extenuations;
smug as a bug
yet never petulant,
really;
happy beyond reproach
or repair
because he doesn't know better.
and about as potent –
the fool –

as a second thought
or a guess
or an unsuccessful flirtation;
the original idea that would never
cross the mind
of the loveable fool
who would never consider confronting the actual.
there is only one truth:
the present is a gift
the past has been wonderful
and the future is laid out in advance.
it will be as told and accepted without question,
and the fool will be happy.

so, when something resembling sense is restored
along with something resembling poetry revealed
the fool's – everywhere – sip humbly and with
little remorse (we can still hope) on apology and silence,
some leftovers and some thoughts in hand;

with some hoping to be felt-up, exclusively,
in the extension of a fool's paradise.

the curse

the curse begins with the desire to write –
and then you don't.
the 'writer' (and we use the term loosely,
 at this point) has nothing but the excuse
not to write
let alone the *great american novel*.
and since when were twenty-four hours
in a day not enough for the lack of inspired
excusing by way of unseen dilemmas?;
for the writer's search for a masculine prose that
connects with the feminine side –
as long as the writer's block desists beyond the thought
that it doesn't even exist.

which begs the question: does writer's block exist?
some in the writing community believe the 'block' is a fallacy;
a form of vain laziness.
this might be true,
but to the struggles of a writer
it feels more like a phobia without a cause or a cure.
it's a gallery of looming, invisible hypochondria seeking
its own shape within the writer's gut and very own head;
a shadowy specter spider-webbing across a semi-closed mind,
teasing in its shroud, and exposing itself for a gratuitous laugh

at the most inopportune time;

or, when easier, the light that shines bright from a

catch phrase or a halcyon day:

> the sun does rise
>
> everyday
>
> even if we don't see
>
> life stumbling
>
> into its imitation.

opa

his children were not even
a glint in oskar's eye
as he stood next to his 1928 motorcycle
with a sidecar for one.
he was soon to travel,
early, the pacific coast highway
and be the subject of a photo in a grassy courtyard
near a tower at berkeley;
and a lasting winter of sun in california;
and more photos would be taken
with german-american compatriots
crowding the sidecar by the motor bike.
and one of oskar's friends, arno,
would tell him to look-up his family when
oskar returned to germany.
and he did in 1930 meeting arno's sister, ilse;
and in 1931 oskar and ilse married;
and, promptly, went back to america and nyc;
and soon a daughter was born; and back to california;
and a son was born in san francisco.
and, then, a change in the work venue
as they moved back east to new jersey
where oskar worked at a growing electrical plant

employed, mostly, by german-americans
that would help in the construction of airplanes –

and the first hint of suspicion of just *who* was oskar working for?

he would never get to ride his motorcycle
across the usa – like he'd planned –
and he never lost his passion for the german homeland
where he, abruptly, returned his wife and kids – in 1939 –
to the chagrin and objections of oskar's brother, alfred,
and other german-americans who tried to warn him
of the politics and the war that more than loomed.
oskar would not listen to his brother or anyone else.
he was adamant.

and oskar would only visit america, after 1940.
he would see his american family three times before
he would pass and there would be some speculation
amongst his grandchildren how he had been capable
of moving back to germany before the start of the war
and then have his two children delivered back to the usa,
again, after ww2 ended: hamburg remained in rubble –
through 1949 – and america was not.

and oskar did not follow his children, this time.
he remained in germany with ilse;
and they divorced; and both remarried.
and his two children grew-up in foster homes
in northeast ohio contacted by letters and
german-influenced christmas's; marzipan and kaspar
and saint nicholas would, eventually, be under the tree

for oskar's grandchildren to see.
the family was protestant and the swedes, also,
had a strong following – the nationalities uniting,
for some time, by religion and the beliefs of martin luther:
'here i stand. i cannot do otherwise,' luther had stated on
behalf of his life, back in 1521.

and, on christmas eve in 1972, the third grandchild –
who was barely aware of being lutheran, at the time –
was asked to recall his grandfather by his german name:
'opa?' had arrived in america to see the grandchildren
and the five-year-old grandson had said it correctly,
and oskar laughed a bellyful that shook with his bag of
german books and steiff puppets
and the old *geige* he used to play.
opa was saint nicholas himself – to the grandchild –
with the white hair and the holiday cheer,
smiling from cheek to cheek hugs.

what might have passed before oskar's eyes?
so far removed from the man who had traveled
with whimsy and little fear the pacific coast highway;
who had managed to travel from japan
by train through siberia to reunite in germany;
and the grandchildren could not help but wonder and ask:
how could a german have traveled from japan *through russia*
to meet his american born children and german born wife in
germany...in 1940?!...could opa have been a spy or a double-agent just
effective enough to keep his children and wife alive...?
from germans and americans?

oskar may never have looked back; or second guessed;
or ever been a spy, german or american; loved the red, white, and black;
cautious of yellow and blue, it might seem.

either way,
that papa-opa twinkle in the eye
remains visible to the five-year-old at heart
believing in the image of his very own,
modern day saint nick.

owning up

it has been said intelligent people
have conversations with themselves.
this is good as long as they are not
schizophrenic.
it also may be more than a theory
that if you think you are going crazy
you are not
because you would, simply, not be aware of the insanity.
that kind of sounds insane.

you may have had these doubts and troubles
and fear of aging perspectives while
drinking heavily during hard times
and it may have prolonged depression.
you may have actually drank or inhaled
or injected stronger drugs in the attempt
to deal with the arts or the poet or the
jesus in your blood,
and managed to maintain control of sanity;
remaining on the brink of that understanding with
enough accomplices to remain on the fringe,
at worse.

you can imagine 'spilling your guts' all over
the place – subjectively;
restructuring the way the world is seen
through common and vacant eyes.
but, this only does you any good because
the conformed are not aware of the
alternate possibilities.
and there you might stand, supposedly,
at rock bottom
climbing from the depths
in front of rows of people,
smoke everywhere,
with the rock bottom – and the smoke – the 'one' thing in common;
and the conventional no place to go but up
improvement.

so, if nothing else,
we all remain the proud owners
of our self-titled
humanity.

a collage and an 8-track

it was an attempt to separate
from the fuel of repetition:
a moment of dependence
in music and song,
quoting and singing
to one's self – especially in private –
ended.
the user had abused the format
long enough;

poetic infusion revitalizing
the justice in the one-time colleague,
held in part by working the one side
of an 8-track, blues tape
from *deep in the woods*;
a suburbanite
no more, really;
no longer able to
avoid the sounds of
misplacement;
when 'pushing the limits'
of question
is stalling, and late,
to the tardiness and strain

of, barely, pushing 30;
of the gut feeling
of the not-so-revealing
politicos campaign to believe
their con

while, inevitably, losing the woman
of his dreams
to the town
and the complicit
strength of city hall;

and the right to that freedom
to think, openly,
made him different,
in their eyes;
and her too:
why care as long as he
continues to place the gun
to his own head?

hypocrisy turning into people
conforming too seriously;

that his freedom evolved
against the town,
not too far removed from the 'blues and the woods',
is him remaining true to form
and not forgetting
what they all used to believe in,
now deferring for the sake of agreement.

and the non-conformer took his back seat
and turned the tv on
and watched the end of a 'good ol' boy,' southern
red neck movie racing cars and beating the cops
and delivering the moonshine to people who deserved it
more than the 'bull crap' law and the local sheriff and his
inept deputies deserved to enforce.
and the non-conformist did not feel very productive,
again, for doing very little and wasting his time
watching the car crashing slapstick, tobacco
chewing, not too far from the woods nonsense,
in explosive fire and color.
it had been originally released in 1978 and it could not
have come – to the non-conformist – at a worse time.
it seemed like a waste of time and visual print
so counter-productive he thought about dismantling
his 8-track but, somehow, that seemed more destructive
than all the car jumps and the extra crashes and all those
possible takes.
he continued not too listen,
but left the 8-track alone
with the thoughts of that girl –
in what used to feel like his hometown –
working for the mayor
in city hall.

alternate ego eccentrics

'do you believe in god?' he thought he innocently asked her.

'it must suck to be you,' she suddenly said.

'did i miss something?'

'no, you've been here the whole time…got anything else to say?'

'did I offend you?' he felt somewhat bloated, spewing some alcohol, barley, and hops from his system.

'you're too insignificant to offend me.'

'maybe you need a drink?'

'no, i don't.'

'why are you in a bar…?

'none of your business.'

'you must have a boyfriend.'

'i said, none of your business.'

'are you an atheist…?'

'i didn't say that.'

'are you angry with god for not having a boyfriend?

'fuck you.'

'oh, you're catholic….'

'have another drink.'

'more of the devil's water, please…are you buying?'

'not for you….'

'if you're trying to get in my pants it's not working.'

'you wish,' she said.

'i don't wish for too many things anymore.'

'who do you think you are?'

'just me.'

'good luck with that.'

'thanks, and you too with that catholic-atheist, no boyfriend dilemma.'

'what?'

'you can leave anytime now.'

'yes, so can you…'

'goodbye…nice talking to you…' he didn't leave.

'go fuck yourself.'

'that's not fun…probably be more fun to watch you fuck yourself.'

'that's you, pervert.'

'why are you still talking to me?' he laughed and thought, briefly,

about walking away but could not deny he was enjoying himself.

'you can go now…' she said.

'you need to find a boyfriend or god…or become a nun

 …or a born again christian…something…'

'fuck you…you don't know. '

'we all gotta' start somewhere…'

she was silent, hesitant in her grace…

'it's not too late for a drink, baby.' he suggested, again.

…followed by what appeared to be a flash of her middle finger.

'is that a vow of silence or celibacy, honey?'

she was quickly escorted by her two girlfriends to a table at the

far end of the bar.

'she's not your baby or your honey,' one of her friends yelled back.

at this point he was well aware of this.

he could not help but wonder, though, if the one girlfriend who had

not spoken seemed amused.

van gogh deserving

is the same as a poet's heart
discovering itself
in the subtleties of life;
caustic, and the belief,
in the colors
and the art;

dreaming all those insane
dreams
and the golden colors
from the movies
that vincent may have thrived on
in his day,
if a motion-picture camera
existed.

but, those dreams
loomed like lepers
in his head
ringing in his ears
like an endless contribution
toward emotion and the poor;
golden lepers of insanity

chopping-off whatever can't
be digested in one man's soul
of a lifetime;
searching for the next

starry night
over the pool table
in our very own room of

disproportion;

a red wall, yellow blossoms
and golden sunlight
alive and well
in the 19th century
of his today.

television paint

the colors tend to run
together
in a blood stream
and a baffling brook –

towards murder!
it's like
some kind a life
on tv

and all, usually,
comes together in a sprightly
conclusion,
within the hour;
the telly

changing over the years
with some graphic gloss
hopefully reminding us
we are not a part
of the massive mess;
somewhat
brainwashing the lot

in its odd,
at the fingertip, less than
static meetings

with people not really known;
originating and familiar to us
from the beginnings of our viewing days,
with that english standard sub plot, also;

praising with a hail,

in their way,
'it's only pop tv culture.'

native land/native trust

the old western pact;
the land and
dust and the
rock like sun;
authentic, yet, a license
of its own beautific mettle

from its panoramic
history; archaic
beauty and far the reach
of its deaths;
the wild horse must feed
on water;
its soul, raw;
the buffalo range avoids the lizard
and chameleon paint snaking through
borrowed canyon; vultures both;

the canyon – another planet –
stoned-turquoise
and bleeding high;
a red moon
and river, in the beginning,
flowing; void;

less peyote hallucinate;
but wanting;
more, finding the inner beast child;
closure of land, soul

and the call of a native's name
echoing its prescience.

a speakeasy

a toast
to the good and the bad;
to 'saying it like it is...'
like a shot of adrenaline
shooting to the center of the brain
away from a bad hangover or migraine
waiting
to levitate and, slowly,
float away
like a pain-free suicide
gone awry;
to another invisible place
involving breathless air,
not so complete
and wondering if
the questions, floating, without design
could be stable
or true

to
a final say
to the final completion
to the longest poem ever written

over and over
by someone else
because there is that creative belief
existing in the streams behind the conventional mind
that permanence is success
to the one that also believes the 'end all be all'
is not just writing
but art and life and death, together;
that this plural word phrasing is not to be
dismissed as taboo.

even the impractical artist, out of his or her element,
oddly aims to please
while pissing on their own marginal souls
and zipping-up in the face of others;
considering waiting for someone to call the 'phony in the rye'
out of complete seclusion
or that other guy
no longer 'on the road'
away from his mother
(far too late, now, for those concerned);
for the, sometimes, misinterpreted impractical artist
the lie seems to get bigger
(and you know what 'they' say about 'the bigger the lie...?
 the more people believe');

hypocrisy nursing
the not so hypocritical
to drink

and consume behind these
closed doors
just to save some face
and cool it down,
for a spell.

the recurring theme of drink

men and women
drink together
in portent's lounge
with relaxed, intoxicating smiles
well aware of losing their perspective
on things;
aware of being bent
away from the left or the right
like good drinking philosophers should;
staid in the center
of inebriation
not disbelieving in god,
or believing in the devil only in spirit or metaphor;
dark red with the deceiving knowledge of ivory circles
above the horns;
and fringes and linings of other possible colors
mingling in the crowd, testing the boundaries,
in a mixture of the senses
because you, finally, experience something
others don't:
'you're on to something,' as the creator says
understanding, relating, feeling the experience
you knew deep down could be brought to the surface
without creating the argument.

the argument, unavoidably, is handed to you
in the artful form
of the life
on a silver platter
that loves yourself and those who love in return
(a special little trick that god laid upon us with a wink
 and a devil's smile on his face).

sleep space

an inquiring seductress
she is
in the back of a man's mind,
again, once upon the silence of another day's
buried conversations
awakened by the possible memory of a
self-hypnosis surviving
the slow-motion death scene
of diving into a large pool of some
significant substance;
an intoxicating, unpredictable freedom fall
to any soul
sleepwalking through an occasion a sight more feasible
than the last day
or the last dream;
certainly not plausible but a lesson in itself;
the dream of the past with a sense of reality;
something to remember
something to improve on;
the, sometimes, indescribable mish-mash of mental euphoria:
good, bad, ecstatic, horrific these
continual mental news flashes of burning light brought to us in all their
extravagant questionable colors
and black and white

that 'gave-up' eons ago trying to resemble an exact utopia
or a pure hell
(with a nod to realities strength and longevity);
simply cognizant of a place where the rhyme or possible prophecy
in a dream has quietly succumbed to reason

in a space
maybe not so wide or grand,
but existing.

the cleanliness of film

we are sometimes surprised by what
we see in the movies
even when
we believe we have seen it all.
but, why else would an actual director
say he was not impressed with the work
of gary cooper
until what he saw of him
on film.
somehow, and
for some reason,
the camera just loved the guy.
or someone like michelle pfeiffer
saying
she would rather hide in the corner of a room
away from people;
unimpressive socially
yet 'stars', these people, resembling us and
speaking to us with the help of a good voice
and a good director.

movies can scare us even if it is not a horror film.
they scare people because they can take ninety minutes
from our lives

just like that.

it's good to realize/to understand/to remember/

that being miserable or happy is a communal commodity

and that a truly inspired movie with a director's inspired image

can bring so many bright minded individuals thinking together.

sometimes, the most stimulating movies are about people

and their emotions – sometimes artistic emotions;

and these movies, without outrageous explosions

or outlandish special effects, could have been made by us;

we feel we could have written that or we –

at the right moment and in the right mood –

could have acted in that manner (with the right direction, of course).

we begin to wonder if we could have 'done better'.

and there's coop laying it all on the line, again,

still fighting for what he believes in,

at *high noon*; his puritan wife in waiting.

and

suzie diamond is a scene in her own right

rolling on the piano and singing in a

smooth tight, red satin dress;

a lounge-smoking glittery performance

indeed.

her piano player lover would turn his emotional back on her

and she would walk away, in the end.

'don't you forsake me oh my darlin,'

we are told again,

in time with the movies.

proper channels

what takes place on the job
is almost like fighting over
what's on the tv;
people ordering on demand
the show most convenient
and cost efficient
to them;
(remote please, changing channels)

the inevitable hypocrisy
of politics;
democracy gone republican.
(same old news, tv or radio)

'the plight of mankind is at the hands
 of people who have the guts
 to make the hardcore decisions
 so don't worry about it,'
a radio dj says
calling himself the 'cheese and rice' of the airwaves,
tongue in cheek, nail in cross.
(the dial turns)

how come the picture's so grainy? we have cable.
this is not hd.
oh.
(remote again, changing channels)

sometimes things are just not clear enough on tv
to be heard,
not even on media day;
the point beaten over our heads;
the picture, like our fellow employees, more imaginative,
graphic and mostly censored.
so don't be fooled,
channel surfing employees,
searching for proper channels:
the will of man may never change.

the three graces

pretty much as straight
as their names
on this one night:
dawn, june, and an eve.
they sat in their triangular circle
backs to the bar
legs crossed in flowers and dresses
watching what was and what
might be
play out in front of them
while smiling at each other
some;
watching, comparing, impressing
upon the lives and old friends
they had not seen in years;
easily reminiscing
lively and calm;
well aware
of drinks
and a future
never forced;
laughing, adjoining –
the graces watched –
from their seats;

tan shoulders

shining through;

having another one of their

superior nights

while in the fold

sipping on life

as it comes to them

always

in their soft, genuine effort.

omega moonlight

who knows how long
it will last?
the words lost
somewhere in night
of a crescent fold

with no story to be told;
behold! no beginning
or end (for now);
looking up

or down;
plagiarizing the night
eclipse, the thought,
wide asleep;

the dark side of
the silhouette
with points
flat in its
distance
turns,

somehow,
on its shadow
departing the view

with a leveled idea
and a blink

the moon is an outline
and gone.

cid in america

there was this spanish patriot
on tv
who fought against the moors
on tv
and it's considered an american
classic.
if you can see it on widescreen
tv
it's supposed to be even better.

charlton heston portrayed the
title character
and no one over acted as well as
mr. heston.
while watching, though,
i could not help but think about
michael moore
and the documentary he made
in america
about gun control
and the interview he managed
to conduct with an elderly
charlton heston.
it had been difficult to watch

the one time all-american man

from all those movies about the bible,

in all their power and all their glory;

and the pride of spanish integrity,

and the 'planet of the apes'

made in america.

it was almost comic

but mostly tragic

how an image had changed

for a man who believed in the right

to bear arms.

and there was michael moore placing the photo

of the little girl who was shot in school

by a six-year-olds choice

as an ancient charlon heston

walked away from the interview.

remembering how chuck had been documented

sucked so bad

i had to turn off the 11th century spanish legend

portrayed by charlton heston

pretty much made famous

in america.

but, let me not forget about sophia loren

the curvaceous, italian international star

who could not live with

the spanish legend

on tv

because he had been forced
to kill her father in a dual of honor
and purely primal, 11th century political beliefs.

rumor has it there were real tensions between
sophia loren and charlton heston
that may have helped their strained love scenes
together.

i wonder how sophia ever felt about gun control.

martin scorcese has been quoted saying
el cid is the last of the great epics
from the hollywood film industry
which may force me to watch again,
under a different italian-american light.

burning bridges

the past, for now,
is a living breathing,
practically smoldering,
memory that may not matter
in the long run.
the stories will always bare witness, somewhere.
the books open and shut.
there is so much that happened
to the ones we thought we knew.
politics, religion, jobs, nepotism:
'people have been to bed with...'
and they don't even realize it,
the 'motherfuckers.'
and you always have to be careful what you say
in public or at work.
the things that usually make
for better print are forbidden.
either way, it shouldn't matter
what side of the bridge you're on.
you can see it coming, in time.
you can feel it, with age.
and when you ignore the smoke signals
it's easy to get burned.

more than one bridge is a cinder,

these days.

does it change anything

beneath the surface of a recently razed, burnt-out bridge

to the simple puss

who was once thought

to be just

biding the time

trying not to be vindictive

awaiting the next inevitable,

bluesy crossroads to cross

without any more incidents?

or the understanding from a song writer's

unusual lyric:

'hey, baby, i got statistics i got stats

these people have been to bed...'

figuratively difficult to ignore;

the nice guy,

careful what to say,

somehow stuck

like a third degree prick

on the other side

of twenty-odd years

of a burning metaphor;

like kindling from the page

ready to rekindle a kindred...

or spirit something

a. walther

without hands?

sometimes,
it's the only way to learn.

eternal witness/constant observer

the meeting was a one-on-one.
not a confrontation
mind you
just a meeting between two people:
one a college educated, county employee
and the other, well,
myself.
unemployment had brought us together
following a three hour 'orientation' in a room with twenty others,
unemployed, plus three employed speakers and a video the county
had supplied.
we sat in his open cubicle
shook hands
and looked at his computer screen at the possibility of employment
with the proper application and resume instruction.
'says here you believe you need computer skills.'
'yes, i'm a dinosaur when it comes to computers.'
'no e-mail address?'
'no, no e-mail address.'
'you have a computer?'
'yes. I write on it, a lot.'
'what do you write?'
'uh, um…creative writing…something resembling poetry…'
blank stare.

'i considered that for a title,' but i did not elaborate.
i felt like i'd lost him.
'do you have a family to support?'
'no, lucky i guess.'
'what kind of work are you looking for?'
'i've got a sample of my writing here…'
'what we're you doing before you came here?'
'i'd been a shuttle bus driver…nothing hard to find, so i thought,
 till I got laid off.'
'why were you laid-off?'
'cutbacks, downsizing,' not exactly the truth but not a lie either.
he, probably, knew this already and did not feel i needed to elaborate
that it was probably more personal and complicated than just a
corporate business decision.
no blank stare, this time.
and he talked for the most part of a half-an-hour telling and showing me
on his computer where i might be able to find some work 'in my field'
in the cleveland area.
schooling, of course, became an option; computer skills more and more
a necessity; an e-mail address a good place to start.
very little was said about my writing skills – or lack of.
'ok, you can go now…it's lunch time…somebody else will contact you
 within two weeks…remember, contact two employers a week while you
 are receiving unemployment benefits.'
'ok…and who will contact me?'
'somebody from the ohio department of job and family services.'
good gig, i thought, at least unemployment is keeping somebody employed.
and, as i left the building, just in time for lunch, there were business
skirts and suits walking up and down 9th street.
there were some dressed much more casual, kind of like myself,
in jeans or shorts and t-shirts with a slogan or a sports team proudly

and innocently on display.

i was not sure what the five youths were doing hanging-out on the street

corner across from the sunoco station.

they seemed to be asking too many questions of the passers-by.

i was home within fifteen minutes after exiting 9th street.

eleven miles on the freeway with no concern for rush hour traffic is,

practically, cause for celebration

and a quick drive.

the sun was out and the lake almost looked blue beyond the break walls

and the shoreline.

and, then, there was nothing much to do, but wait for a call

and watch the usual

and fill-out applications on line because this is a computer age.

and i did not mention the city allowed free parking for the unemployed.

that was nice.

it was free as long as there was a space available in the parking garage

attachment.

i may have been fortunate to find a space amongst the 'reserved'

for employee parking spaces and the other unemployed personnel who had,

also, attended 'seminars' and had arrived for their own, semi-personal,

one-on-one 'counseling'.

i suppose the most fortunate one will be whoever is re-employed first.

against the all-mighty

so much has turned/turned
to a derogatory statement.
what had once seemed 'life'
has taken a new meaning.
it is all nothing, really,
when you think about it.
and nothing extraordinary, either.
but, it is against all (or most)
of what we thought it would be,
from the start,
the elusive 'meaning of life' question
that may not be deserving
of an answer;
the stem of its indecision
inconsistency.
but, once again, it is like a tempest
that has nothing to do with climate,
or the feeling of running nowhere
headlong against 'it all';
the future not so scientific.

ah, the not so proverbial world

sure does spin

a bit top heavy, on its axis,

until, sometime,

you just might swear

you can sense that rotation

almost begging to stop.

but, of course, that won't happen

in this/our lifetime;

not in this/our turn

at the rotation.

inside the box/balancing the scales

a collection of ideas
brought to the forefront
is, by theory, a practice.
suspicion, it seems,
attempts to defend peculiarities
in lieu of reason.
and the definition of logic,
in turn,
becomes as confusing as a crisis.
not very personable,
these walls;
seclusion intervening with
a spirit and care all its own;
the soul only recognizable
from the inside,
not out,
for no one to see.
sort of inhuman,
the tendency here,
when one thinks about it;
nearsighted
when the properties of a ghost and a recluse
apply themselves
together;

often a cold comfort;
silver chains on a rustic scale
weighing things openly and unevenly;
hiding, the senses,
from a questioning view
inside the box.
outside,
sartre and nietzsche can speak to each other
of a play about *zarathustra*, for example;
privy for the world to expose,
for whomever may wish such a thing.
or, if witnessed enough,
for all to believe.

inside or outside the truth be told:
do lies twist the soul
or is it just the beginning
of common knowledge?

when in need

when in need
look at a page number
or something else self-effacing
because sometimes
even the poem never
begins
like it was intended

like when
it was important to dream
and wish upon things
that seemed uniquely and innocently
and, quite frankly, improbable or immature
yet important
to a child who was
'going to be'
a princess or astronaut or president
or a million dollar a year baseball player

and like,
you know,
when childhood becomes a teenager
and then thirty something
those earlier intentions tend to be downgraded

to a greyer, starker version of 'one day at a time',

for example:

it was never supposed to turn-out this way

for the dream or the poem,

but when one concedes these dreams or wishes

will not come true

and the posing of a child change to reality

the importance of dreams and their significance

are downgraded to miniscule.

this alteration in perception may be all that's needed

to change the perception of what is meant by success:

fame? wealth? children? grandchildren?

who knows when the feeling of success finally 'sinks-in'

for the rich or the poor.

could it only be in the form of worldwide recognition

especially when it is least expected?

or is it, or should it be, in a more meditative, personal level?

it can't be the same; different people, different times.

'to each their own'

as so many have been known to say

with or without a better ending or page number

to manage or conceive of

struggling in final

word sensation

Author bio

a. walther is a pen name for the author when writing poems.
the immediate excess poems is his first completed volume.
A second book titled *on second thought the work and some progress poems* is in progress and near completion.

a. walther resides where he grew up in northeast ohio

www.ingramcontent.com/pod-product-compliance
Lightning Source LLC
Chambersburg PA
CBHW072024040426
42447CB00009B/1722